O9-BSA-393

Butterflies and Moths

A STUDY OF THE LARGEST AND MOST BEAUTIFUL OF THE INSECTS

by RICHARD A. MARTIN

illustrated by Rudolf Freund,

James Gordon Irving, Eloise Wilkin

GOLDEN PRESS NEW YORK

 Designed and produced by Artists and Writers Press, Inc. Printed in the U.S.A. by Western Printing and Lithographing Company. Published by Golden Press, Inc., New York. Published simultaneously in Canada by The Musson Book Company, Ltd., Toronto.

Library of Congress Catalog Card Number 61-5443

Cloudless Sulphur
Arctic Skipper
Banded Purple
Diana Fritillary
Spring Azure
Parnassian

Summertime

Summer is the time to watch for butterflies. Then, when fields are green and gardens are gay with flowers, the butterflies fly in every sunny place—big butterflies and little ones, dark ones, white ones, and bright-colored ones. Some are as blue as the sky, some as yellow as sunshine. Some have spots or speckles of different colors on their wings, others broad bands or narrow stripes. Still others have wings with strangely shaped markings.

Butterflies are creatures of the daytime. Many of them fly only when the sun is bright. If a cloud comes between the earth and the sun, a butterfly may quickly come to rest and wait for the sun to shine again. Not many butterflies ever fly after the sun goes down.

At dusk, moths come swiftly to the garden, fluttering about from plant to plant. Like tiny helicopters they hover over each flower, and then are gone as quickly as they came.

Most moths hide in the daytime and fly at night. The beautiful colors many of them have are lost in the darkness.

It seems strange that so many of them should fly toward lights at night. Often they swarm about street lights on warm summer evenings and flutter on the window screens trying to reach

*The **Zebra Swallowtail** is easily recognized by its large size, black and yellow stripes, and its long tails. Swallowtails are the largest butterflies in the United States. The biggest one in this family has a wingspread of 4 to 5½ inches.*

the lamp inside. Moths may even fly right into the open flame of a candle.

Most butterflies and moths live from four to six weeks, but a few live for many months, and others, only two or three days.

The biggest moths and butterflies live in tropical regions. They may be 11 inches across—with their wings spread out—like the giant Atlas moth of India. The smallest moths, like the tiny golden pygmy that lives in England, measure less than a quarter of an inch. The biggest butterflies weigh hundreds of times as much as the little pygmy blue.

Wings may be smooth-edged or fringed, or jagged, or even tailed. There are broad, round wings, and narrow, pointed ones.

Many moths and butterflies have common names that tell their color or their markings. Still others are named from what they eat, how big they are, where they live, or when they fly.

The dog-face butterfly gets its name from the markings on its wings. The pattern makes a rough picture of the head of a dog.

The pygmy blue earns its name of "pygmy" from its small size. The "blue" is a little misleading. The pygmy

Black Witch

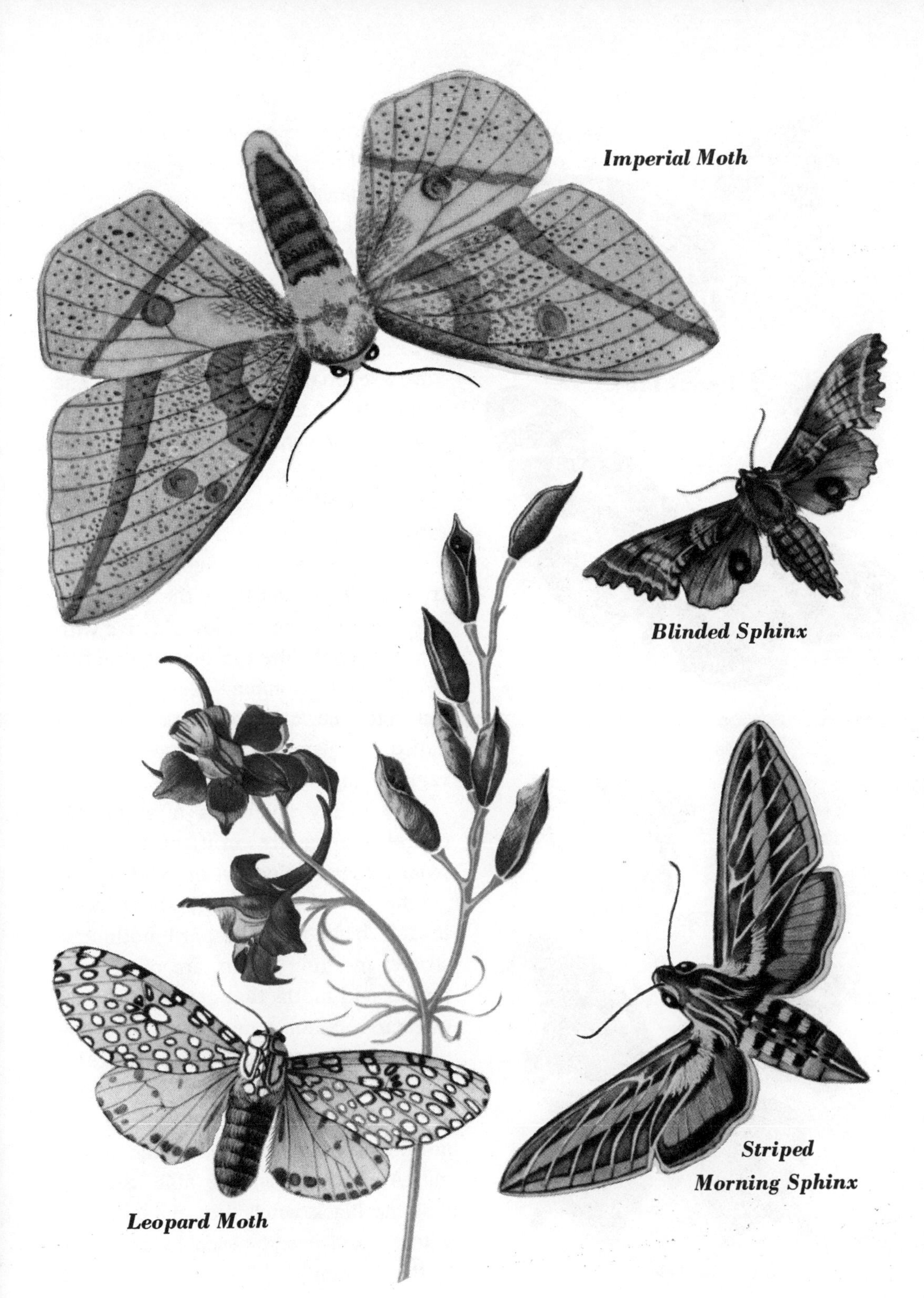
Imperial Moth
Blinded Sphinx
Striped
Morning Sphinx
Leopard Moth

Dog-face Butterfly
Pygmy Blue
Zebra Butterfly
Cabbage Butterfly
Question-mark

blue belongs to a group of butterflies called "blues," but many are more brown than blue.

The zebra butterfly gets its name from its stripes. Sometimes it is called the yellow-barred heliconian.

The small white cabbage butterfly is a common sight in gardens and fields where cabbage is being raised. The caterpillar of this pretty white butterfly also eats broccoli, mustard, and other relatives of the cabbage family, unfortunately, and is a serious pest to vegetable farmers.

The question-mark gets its name from a silvery mark on the underside of each hind wing. A close relative with a mark much like the question-mark's is called the "comma." Both the comma and the question-mark are also called "anglewings" because of their ragged, angular-shaped wings.

The gaudy sphinx is a moth. Of course, the "gaudy" in its name comes from the gay colors on its hind wings.

The cloudless sulphur, zebra swallowtail, black witch, leopard moth, and striped morning sphinx are other butterflies and moths that get at least part of their common names from their appearance. The names "black witch" and "striped morning sphinx" tell even more. You would know that the striped morning sphinx flies about in the morning. And you should be able to guess that the black witch flies at night. No witch would ever be seen flying about in the daytime!

Gaudy Sphinx

You would expect the cloudless sulphur to be yellow, and the leopard moth to have spots.

Learning to recognize a certain kind of moth or butterfly may be harder than you might guess. For you must know the appearance of the underside as well as the upper side of the wings. Besides, one moth or butterfly may occasionally look quite different from another of the same kind. Sometimes the male and female are quite different in appearance. You can see from the picture that the male Io moth is smaller than the female. It has, moreover, bright-yellow

Some butterflies and moths may look unalike even among the same species.

Io Moth

Marine Blue

Fall Cankerworm

bright form

*In some regions, female **Tiger Swallowtails** have yellow and black stripes, while in other areas these butterflies are brown.*

dark form

forewings. The female cankerworm moth does not look like a moth at all. She has no wings!

Not many people would guess that the two pictures of the marine blue are pictures of the same butterfly. The upper and undersides of its wings are very different in color.

The tiger swallowtails shown on this page are both females. But in some regions the female is yellow with black stripes. In other regions the female is brown. Everywhere, the male tiger swallowtail looks much like the yellow-striped female. But the male is smaller.

A great many moths and butterflies have no common names. But scientists have given each moth and butterfly a name that describes each species exactly, so that there is no mistaking one kind for another. Scientific names, too, tell a great deal about the moths and butterflies that have them, but to understand what they tell, you must under stand Latin. They are all Latin names.

An Age of Insects

The time in which we are living might be called the Age of Insects. No wonder, for there are more kinds of insects in the world than all other kinds of animals put together. Scientists have identified about 850,000 different kinds, of which more than 100,000 are butterflies or moths.

The chart below shows the main groups of insects. The moths and butterflies together form one of these groups.

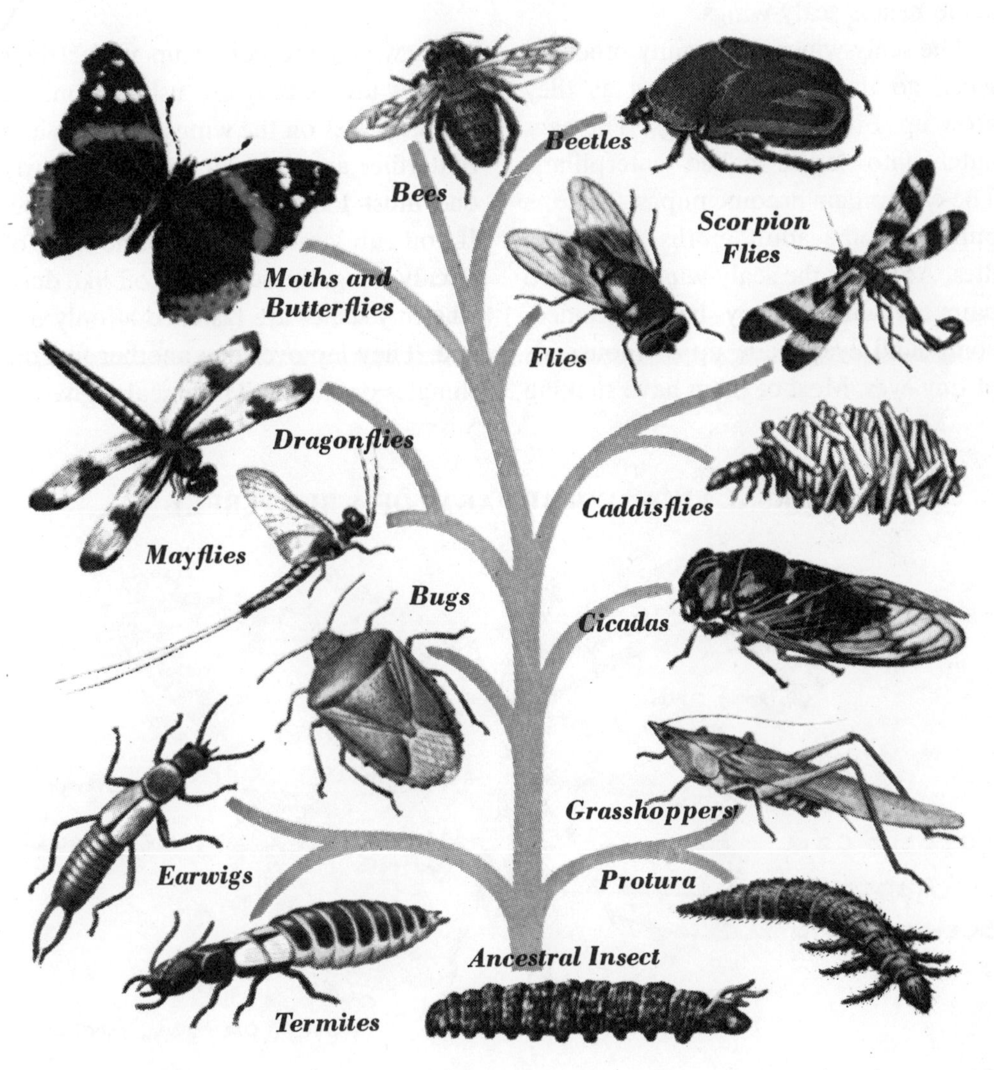

The Scaly-Wings

All butterflies and most moths have sucking tubes coiled up, as part of their mouths. Uncoiled, the tubes make long "sipping straws."

Like all insects, butterflies and moths have six legs, a body divided into a head, thorax, and abdomen, and one pair of feelers, or antennae. They are different from all other insects in having scales on their wings. Scientists have named moths and butterflies Lepidoptera. The name means scaly-wings.

The scaly-wings, like many other insects, go through four stages as they grow up. First, they are eggs. The eggs hatch into larvas called caterpillars. The caterpillars become pupas. And the pupas become adult moths or butterflies. As adults the scaly-wings have two pairs of wings. They have rounded, compound eyes made up of thousands of tiny eyes. Most of them have sucking tubes which are coiled up under their mouths unless they are using them.

The scales on the wings of moths and butterflies are tiny. To see them clearly one must look through a microscope. If you rub your finger over the wing of a scaly-wing, the scales rub off like dust. The tiny scales are fastened at only one end. They lap over one another like the shingles on a roof. These scales give the

DORSAL VIEW OF THE PARTS OF A BUTTERFLY

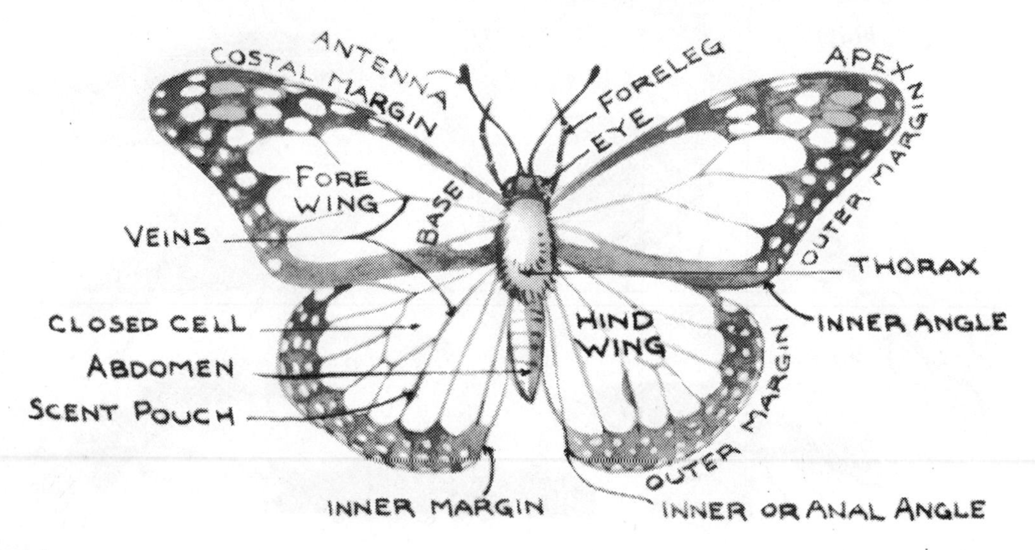

The ***Red-spotted Purple*** *butterfly has a three-inch wingspread, and has bright red spots along the edges of its wings.*

wings of moths and butterflies their beautiful shimmering colors.

Moths and butterflies are often hard to tell apart. But there are differences between them that help to identify them.

One important difference, of course, is the time when they fly. A scaly-wing you see flying about in the daytime is very likely to be a butterfly. One you see after dark is likely to be a moth. But since there are some moths that fly in bright sunshine and a few butterflies that fly at twilight and long after dark, the time you see it flying is not a sure way of telling whether a scaly-wing is a moth or butterfly. However, added to other characteristics of each kind of scaly-wing, this one will help to identify a specimen as either moth or butterfly.

Here are some other characteristics of each group:

A scaly-wing resting on a twig with its wings held out flat is likely to be a moth. One with its wings held straight up from its body is likely to be a butterfly. But this way of telling moths from butterflies is not always certain, either.

The body of a moth is usually stout. Its head may be so close to its body that you cannot see where it begins. Butterflies are usually slender. Their heads are easy to see.

The ***Great Spangled Fritillary*** *rests on a twig with its wings held straight up.*

The huge ***Polyphemus*** *moth is over five inches across. The eyespots on its wings caused it to be named after a mythical one-eyed giant.*

The best way of telling moths from butterflies is to look at their antennae. The antennae of butterflies have club-like knobs at the end. The antennae of most moths do not have clubs. Some moth antennae are threadlike. Others are toothed or feathery. Some are like tiny plumes.

These ways of telling moths from butterflies are ways of telling adults apart. There is no easy way of telling moth caterpillars from butterfly caterpillars. No butterfly caterpillar is as furry looking as the woolly bear caterpillars of some moths. But many moth caterpillars are as smooth as the smoothest butterfly caterpillar. Both kinds of caterpillar have mouths that can chew, and six real legs near their head.

The pupa of a moth is often wrapped in a silken cocoon. Butterfly pupas are not. But here again moths cannot be told surely from butterflies, for not all moth caterpillars spin cocoons.

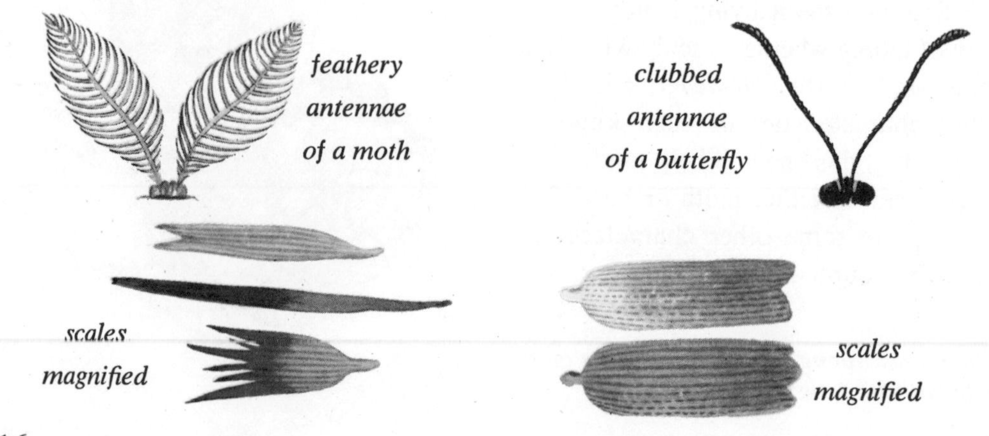

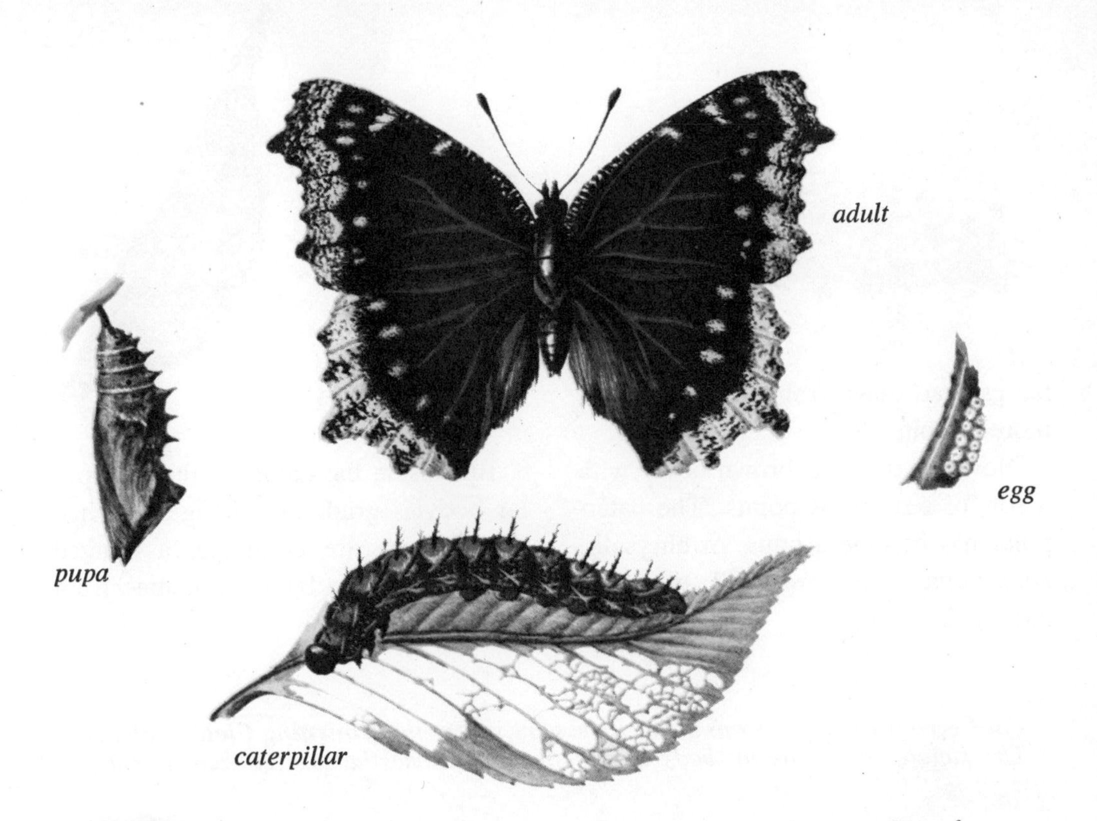

*The **Mourning Cloak** butterfly, like all butterflies and moths, goes through four stages as it grows up: egg, caterpillar, pupa, and winged adult.*

The Story of a Butterfly

Early in the spring, mourning cloak butterflies begin to fly about on warm, sunny days. Soon each female mourning cloak lays her eggs. She lays them in small clusters, usually on willow, elm, or poplar twigs.

The eggs hatch into tiny, prickly-looking black caterpillars, with orange spots down their backs. The little caterpillars line up like soldiers on a leaf and begin to eat. They eat and grow bigger. Soon they are too big for their skins. Each sheds its too-tight skin and gets a bigger one. Changing skins in this way is called molting.

The caterpillars keep on eating and growing. They grow by leaps and bounds. Three more times they molt and each time get new, more comfortable skins. When a caterpillar is full-grown, it stops eating. It fastens itself to a twig with a little button of silk and

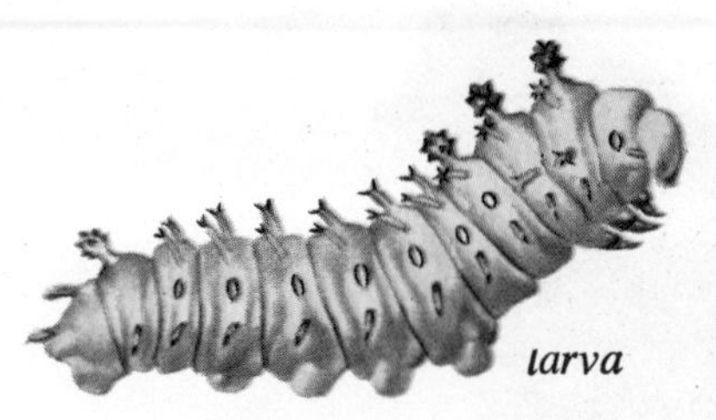

*When the green caterpillar of the **Crecropia** moth is ready to pupate, it attaches itself to a twig and spins a small silken bag for its cocoon.*

cocoon

hangs head down from the twig. Once more it molts.

Now it has a stiff brown cover with a row of red-tipped points. The caterpillar has become a pupa, or chrysalis. As a pupa it stays very still. It neither moves about nor eats.

But inside the chrysalis the caterpillar body is gradually changing. When the changes are complete, a winged mourning cloak butterfly comes from the chrysalis.

*The **Cecropia** moth develops in much the same way as the **Mourning Cloak** butterfly. The picture shows the fat body and feathery antennae that are typical of moths.*

Some moths and butterflies lay a great many eggs close together on one leaf.

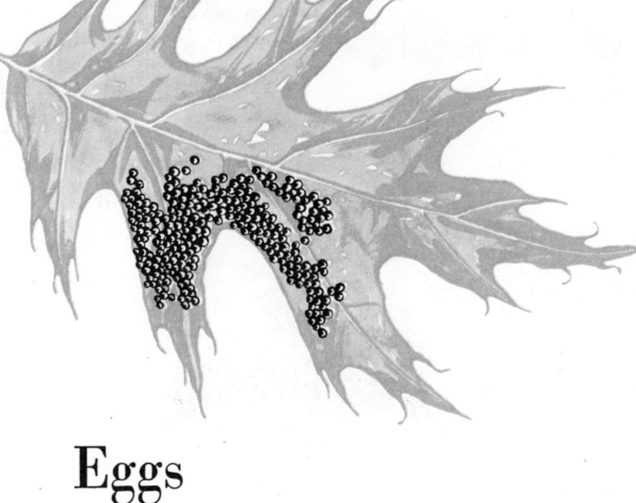

Eggs

"Egg-shaped," if you are talking about scaly-wing eggs, does not mean much. Scaly-wing eggs come in many shapes. The pictures at the bottom of the page show how some scaly-wing eggs would appear if you looked at them under a microscope. In real life, of course, they are much tinier than this. In other ways, however, a scaly-wing egg is like a hen's egg. It has a hard covering, and it holds food for the baby animal inside. A scaly-wing egg is unbelievably small, but it is big enough to hold the tiny caterpillar that hatches from it.

Some butterflies and moths lay their eggs in masses, others in small clusters. Some go from leaf to leaf and plant to plant laying their hundreds of eggs one at a time. The eggs are always laid on the kind of plant that the baby caterpillars will want to eat, after they are hatched. The mother moth or butterfly does not stay to watch over her eggs.

An egg may be round as a berry or flat as a pancake. It may look like a little barrel or a nubby cap. Often there is a beautiful design on the outside of the shell.

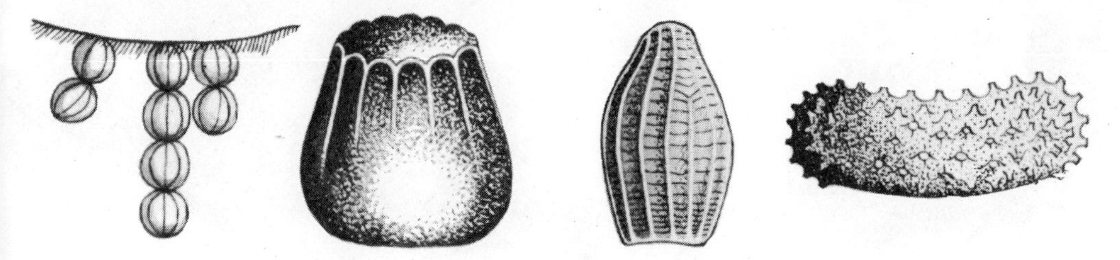

Caterpillars

*Caterpillar of **Luna** moth*

Little caterpillars do not need to be told what to do when they hatch. Almost at once they begin to eat. Ordinarily they do not have to go far to find food, for the mother scaly-wing almost always places her eggs on or near the kinds of plants the caterpillar eats. Some caterpillars eat many different kinds of plants, others only one. The pictures down the side of the page show different kinds of caterpillars and a particular food plant each likes.

Caterpillars live to eat. Their bodies are practically all stomach, for digesting all the food they eat. When they get too big for their skins, they molt. Most of them molt four or five times before they are full grown. After each molt the new skin that the caterpillar has grown may appear to be quite different from the old one.

Black Swallowtail
on parsley

Tiger Swallowtail
on wild cherry

Zebra Swallowtail
on pawpaw

Giant Swallowtail
on orange

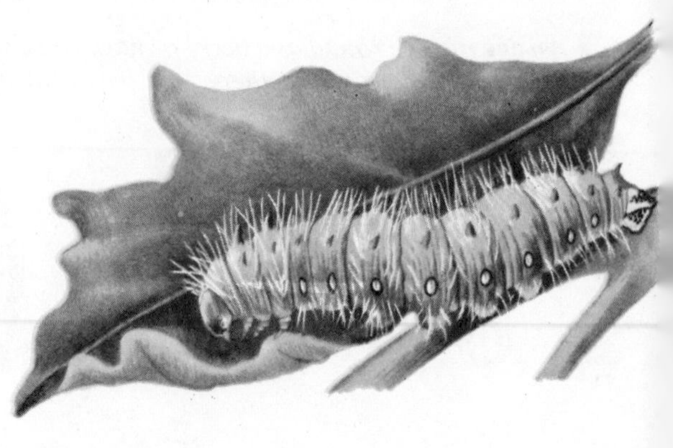
*The hairy caterpillar of the **Imperial** moth eats the leaves of many kinds of trees. Here it is on an oak leaf.*

Full-grown caterpillars may be big or little. They may be brown, black, or bright-colored. A great many are green. They may have spots or bands or stripes or splotches of different colors. Many have horns. Some caterpillars have smooth skins. Others look rough and bumpy. Some are so hairy that they seem to be covered with fur. A few caterpillars have hair or spines which are irritating, if touched.

Caterpillars seem to have a great many legs. Actually, like grownup moths and butterflies, they have only three pairs of true legs. All of a caterpillar's legs except the three pairs near the head are false legs called prolegs. The true legs are attached to the thorax, and the unjointed, false prolegs are on the abdomen, behind the real legs. There may be five pairs of prolegs–one of the five pairs is at the very end of the body – and there may be none at all. Caterpillars that lack some of the prolegs cannot walk in the same way other caterpillars do, but hunch themselves along by arching their backs in a hoop.

Even though caterpillars may look so different, they are all very much alike. Their bodies are made up of rings, or segments. Most have rather large heads with good mouths for chewing plants and with groups of tiny eyes at either side. They breathe through small

The caterpillar of the ***Pearly-eye*** (right), *is as green as the grass it lives on.* Below, ***Cankerworms*** *have only two pairs of prolegs. Because of the way they move, they are often called measuring worms.*

*The **Puss Moth** larva balances itself on its prolegs, raising its head and long tails from its perch.*

holes called spiracles which are located down the sides of their bodies.

Some caterpillars, like the swallowtails, can emit a strong musky odor.

The picture of the Luna caterpillar at the top of page 20 shows plainly many of the different parts of a caterpillar. It is easy to see the segments, the prolegs, the spiracles, and the head and mouth. The tiny eyes do not show, nor, of course, does the all-important stomach inside the plump caterpillar.

*The **Monarch** butterfly caterpillar has long black horns. Its smooth skin is boldly striped in black, white, and yellow. This caterpillar lives on the leaves of the milkweed.*

Cocoons and Chrysalides

The pictures on this page show the pupa stage of seven moths and two butterflies. It is easy to pick out the two butterfly chrysalides. They are much like the chrysalis of the mourning cloak. Of course, the chrysalis of the monarch is a much prettier color. It is green with spots of gold. The pupas of butterflies are called chrysalides because of the golden spots so many of them have. The name comes from *chrysos,* the Greek word for "gold."

All but one of the moth pupas have cocoons of silk. Leaves are woven into some of them. One has the woolly hair of the caterpillar that spun it mixed in with the silk. The pupa of the tomato sphinx moth is quite different from the other moth pupas. It looks much more like a butterfly chrysalis, but it has no golden spots.

When the caterpillar of the tomato sphinx is ready to change to a pupa, it crawls into the ground. A hard brown case forms around it. Many moths that do not spin cocoons go underground when they are ready to become pupas. Sphinx moths have very long tubes for

Butterflies in their resting stage are called chrysalides. Many moths spin cocoons for their pupas, but some may pupate underground. Notice the jug handle on the **Sphinx** *pupa.*

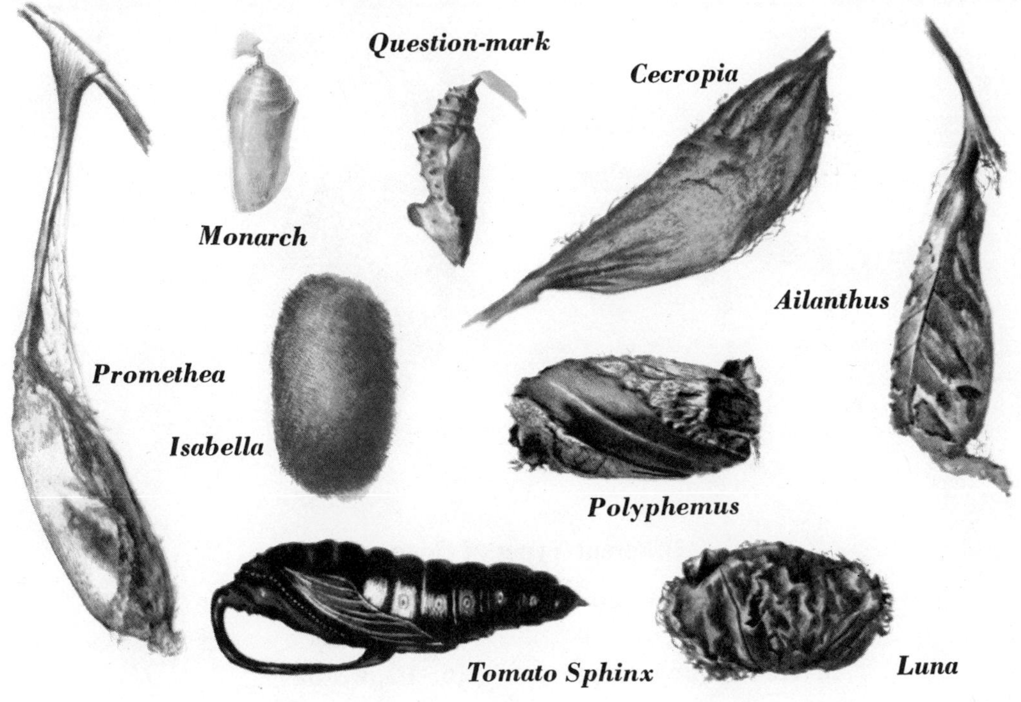

drinking nectar. There must be room in the pupa case for the long tube to develop. The part of the tomato sphinx pupa that looks like the handle of a jug holds the moth's long sucking tube.

The bagworm does not wait until it is ready to become a pupa before spinning its cocoon. It starts to make a bag for itself as soon as it begins crawling about and eating leaves. By the time it is ready for the pupa stage, its bag is big enough to cover it up easily.

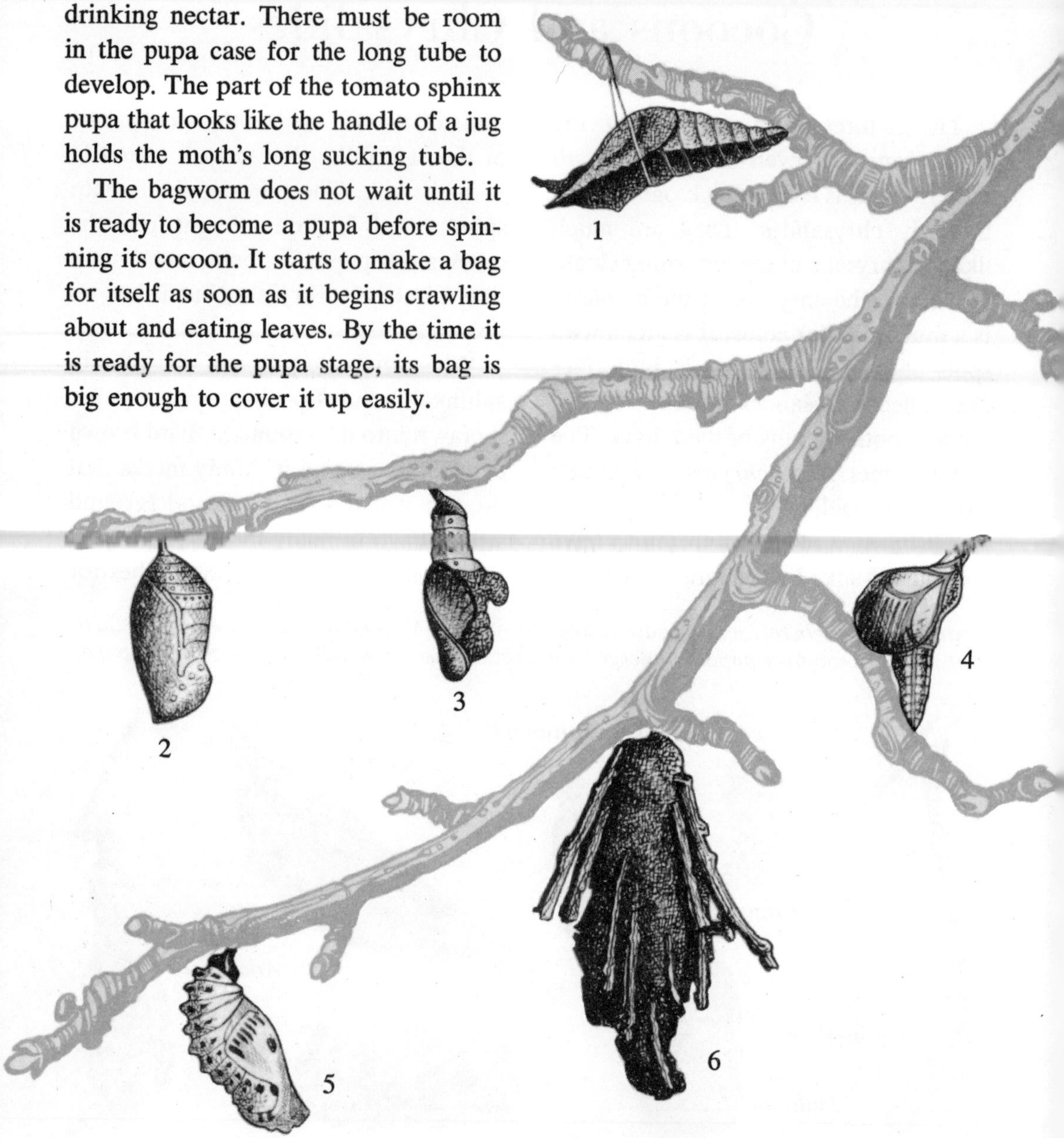

1

2

3

4

5

6

Different Types of Cocoons

1. Spicebush Swallowtail
2. Monarch
3. Red-spotted Purple
4. Cloudless Sulphur
5. Fritillary
6. Bagworm

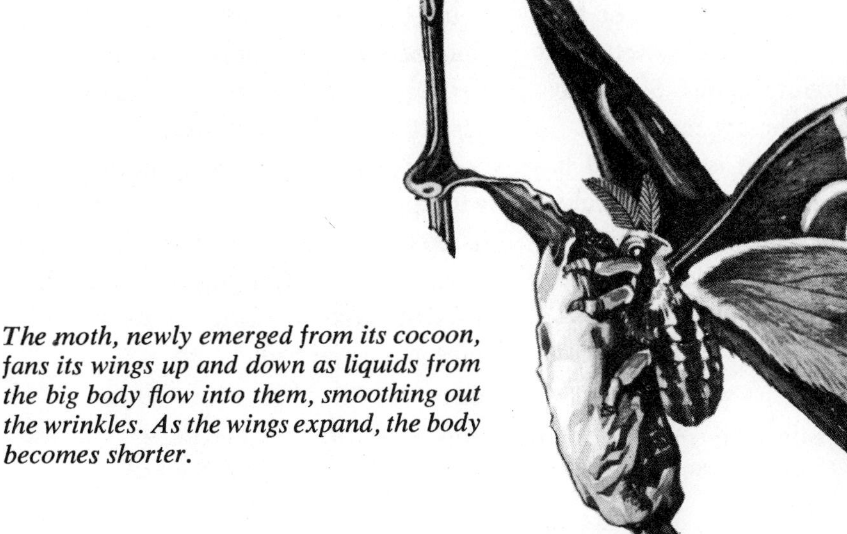

The moth, newly emerged from its cocoon, fans its wings up and down as liquids from the big body flow into them, smoothing out the wrinkles. As the wings expand, the body becomes shorter.

Becoming An Adult

Looking at a cocoon or chrysalis that has dangled from a bare branch all through winter, you will find it hard to believe that shut up in it there is a creature with four big wings. And it is hard to see how the moth or butterfly inside will get out of its tight cover. If it is as beautiful as the ailanthus silk moth, watching it come out from its drab, dry little cocoon is really exciting.

Depending on what kind of moth or butterfly it is, the young insect may stay in the pupa stage for a few days, or for many weeks.

A rustling sound from the cocoon tells that the moth inside is ready. With a liquid from its mouth, it dissolves the silk threads at one end of the cocoon. Then it puts its head through the small opening and wriggles out. Its wings are small and crumpled. Its body is long, soft, and wormlike. The moth clings to a twig and rests.

Soon the moth begins to fan its wings. Liquids from the too-big body flow into them. With the loss of liquids, the body gets shorter. The wings expand and spread out. Their wrinkles disappear. At last there is a moth with strong, beautiful wings. As soon as the wings have dried and hardened, the moth is ready to fly.

Giant silk moths like Ailanthus do not have many days to live after they get their wings. They quickly set about their task of finding mates. Soon after the eggs are laid, the big moths die.

The ailanthus moth is so called because it feeds upon ailanthus leaves. It is a native of Asia, but was brought to America during the Civil War in the hope of setting up a silk industry. Although this proved to be an unsuccessful enterprise, because no cheap method could be found for getting the silk from the cocoon, the moths have flourished here. They are now widespread over the eastern part of the country.

This large, handsome moth has a wingspread of nearly four inches, and its caterpillar is more than two inches long. The moth is a grayish-brown, but has distinctive markings on its wings of olive green and pink.

The feathery antennae of the ***Ailanthus*** *moth help it to find a mate. With its antennae, it can sense another moth of its kind a mile away.*

A Dozen Butterflies

The **Monarch** *butterfly is one of the best-known of all butterflies.*

The monarch is an American butterfly that has spread over the oceans into Europe and Asia, even into Australia. Its caterpillar eats milkweed. One reason the monarch can live in so many different parts of the world is that milkweed grows in so many different places.

In the South and West the buckeye is a very common butterfly. It will dart at other butterflies that come near it and chase them away. The buckeye lays its dark-green eggs on plantain or gerardia. Its caterpillar, too, is dark. The chrysalis is brown.

Anyone might guess that the comma butterfly is a close relative of the question-mark. They are both anglewings. Like the question-mark, the comma has a silver mark on the underside of its hind wings. Its caterpillar may be dark-brown or greenish. Sometimes it is almost white. But whatever its color, it always has many branching spines.

Californians often see the little checkerspot in spring and early summer. Its bristly black caterpillars stay together in colonies. The chrysalis is whitish with brown or black splotches.

The tawny-red regal fritillary has box-shaped silver spots on the underside of its hind wings. It gets the name "fritillary" because of these silver spots.

The **Buckeye,** left, *and its close relatives are often called peacock butterflies.* Below, *the wings of the* **Comma** *look as though someone had chopped notches in them.*

Fritillus is a Latin word that means "dicebox." The regal fritillary caterpillar eats violets. It hides in the leaves during the day and eats at night.

Most butterflies do not have silvery boxes on the underside of their wings. But some are so much like the fritillary butterflies in other ways which do have them that they are named "fritillary," too. The variegated fritillary is one of these. There are no silvery boxes on its wings. This butterfly varies a great deal in size and pattern. One that lives in Nebraska may not look quite like one that lives in Virginia.

"Puddle butterfly" is another name for the common sulphur. Big flocks of this pretty butterfly often sip together from puddles left in country roads after summer rains. The female common sulphur is not so bright a yellow as the male. Sometimes it is white.

The common hairstreak is easy to recognize because of its gray color and the big crimson spot between two hairlike tails on each hind wing. One of the tails is much longer than the other. This butterfly is often called the gray hairstreak. In the West, the underside of its wings may be white. Its dull-green caterpillar looks like velvet.

Of all the butterflies in the United States, the American copper is one of the most common. One reason is that its bright-green caterpillar never has to go hungry. Its food plant, sorrel, is common all over the country. The American copper belongs to a group so-called because of their coppery-red color.

The name "eastern tailed blue" tells a great deal. It is a good name for the little butterfly. The upper side of its wings is blue, and there is a short tail on each hind wing. Many of the butterflies called "blues" are western butterflies. This one lives east of the Rockies.

Variegated Fritillary

The ***Variegated Fritillary*** *and the* ***Checkerspot*** *vary in size and markings. The* ***Regal Fritillary*** *has silvery boxes on the underside of its wings.*

Checkerspot

American Copper

Common Hairstreak

Common Sulphur

Eastern Tailed Blue

Common Wood Nymph

In the West, the ***Common Wood Nymph*** *may lack the bright yellow on its forewings. It belongs to the same family as the six butterflies on pages 27-28.*

The butterfly in the picture is a male. Females have brown wings. The flat, dark-green caterpillar has a brown stripe down its back.

The common wood nymph belongs to a group of butterflies called "satyrs." Most of the satyrs are brown or gray with eyespots on the underside of their wings. Like the satyrs of Greek mythology, many of them live in woods. The common wood nymph caterpillar eats grasses, as do all its relatives.

Almost all swallowtails are big, and most of them are beautiful. The black swallowtail is both. It is very common, too. Its caterpillar eats carrot leaves and parsley. People often smell it long before they see it when they are pulling up carrots. All swallowtail caterpillars give out a strong smell when they are bothered. Most swallowtail butterflies have a tail on each hind wing. Some have none. Some have two on each hind wing. One swallowtail has three.

The female ***Black Swallowtail*** *is darker than this male, and the blue is brighter, and the yellow spots are smaller.*

Cloudy Wing

Arctic Skipper

Skippers

These scaly-wings are all skippers. They get this name because they dart about with sudden starts and stops. There are some 200 kinds of skippers that live in the United States, and approximately 2,000 all over the world.

Skippers are butterflies, but in many ways they are like moths. They fly about in the daytime when skies are bright, just as most butterflies do. And they have butterfly antennae that end in clubs. But their bodies are stout, and they spin a sort of cocoon for their pupas.

These butterflies are spread far and wide over the earth. Most of them are blackish-brown and not very pretty. But the silver-spotted skipper is a beautiful butterfly. Its name comes from the big silvery spots on the underside of its wings. When this butterfly rests, it does not hold its wings quite as most other butterflies do. The hind wings are held somewhat apart from the front wings. Some skippers hold their wings almost flat when they rest, in the way that most moths do.

Skipper caterpillars are smooth. They have big heads and small necks. Those of one group of skippers bore into the roots and stems of yucca and stay there tunneling as they eat. The adult butterflies of the borers are bigger than other kinds of skippers. They are giants, 3 inches across. Another name for yucca borers is "giant skippers."

*The beautiful **Silver-spotted Skipper** is common from Quebec to Panama.*

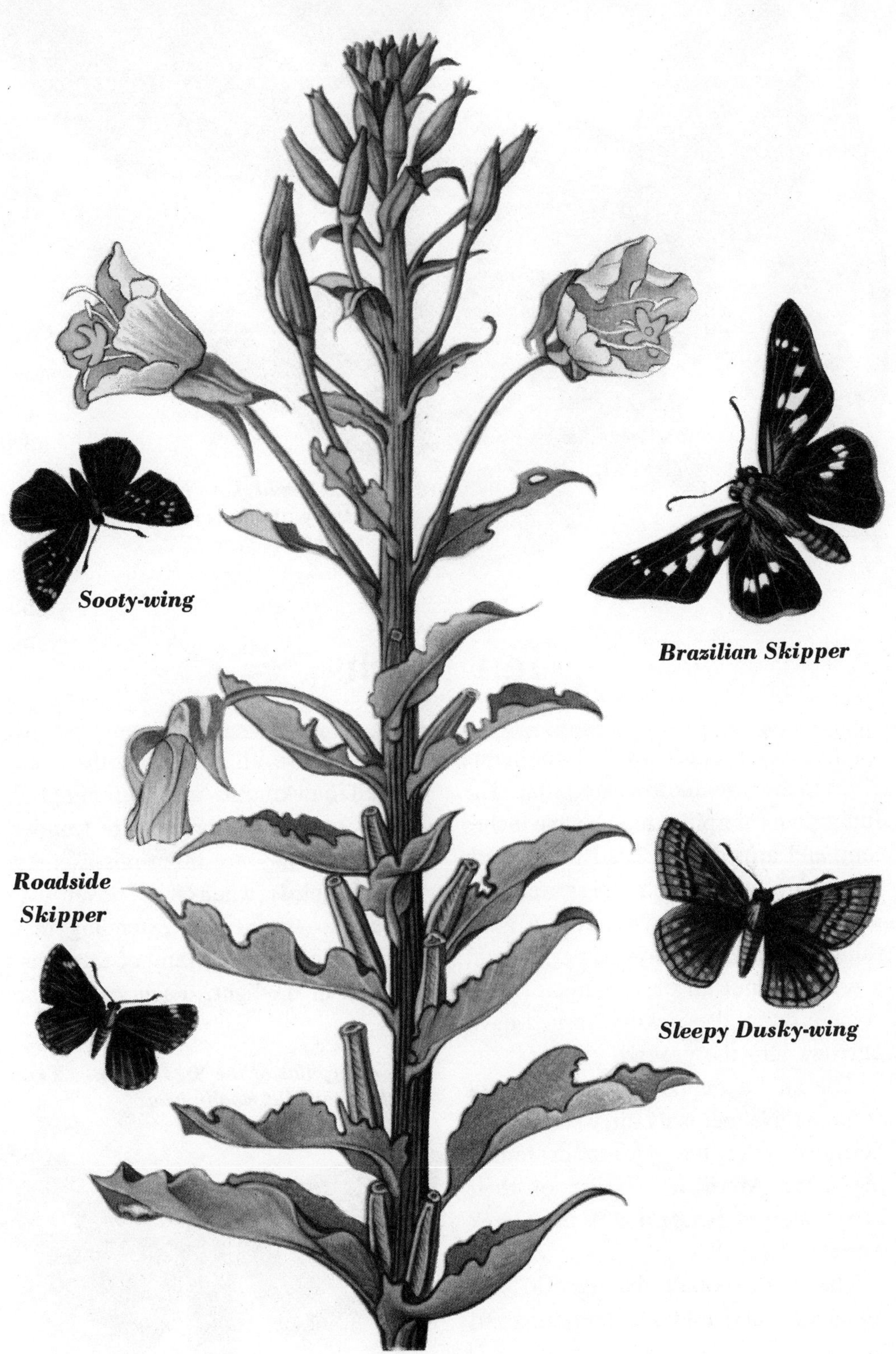
Sooty-wing
Brazilian Skipper
Roadside
Skipper
Sleepy Dusky-wing

The ***Regal*** *moth belongs to the same family as the* ***Imperial*** *moth that is shown on page 9.*

Ten Moths

"Hickory horned devil" is the name given to the regal moth's caterpillar. The full-grown caterpillar may be five inches long and armed from head to tail with long sharp horns. Such a big caterpillar eats a great many leaves. It is a good thing that the moth lays its eggs one at a time and not all on one tree. To become a pupa, the hickory horned devil burrows into the ground.

The St. Lawrence tiger moth is not common. Neither is its furry caterpillar. Scientists gave the tiger-moth family the name Arctiidae because of their furry caterpillars. *Arktos* is the Greek word for "bear."

The pink-spotted hawkmoth, the tomato sphinx, and the hummingbird clearwing are all sphinx moths. They are all hawkmoths and hummingbird moths, too. Sphinx moths are wonderful flyers. They are often mistaken for hummingbirds when they hover over flowers to sip nectar, extending their long sucking tubes. Many of them visit gardens in daylight. Their caterpillars

The caterpillar of the ***St. Lawrence Tiger*** *moth is called a woolly bear.*

earned for them their name of "sphinx." The odd way the caterpillars hold their heads when they rest reminded people of the Egyptian Sphinx.

Because of the soft green color and the graceful lines of its wings, many people think that the Luna moth is the loveliest of all the moths and butterflies. The Luna is big, but it is not nearly so big as some of its relatives. The Hercules moth, a relative in Australia, may measure ten inches when its wings are spread out. The Luna caterpillar is quite common on persimmon trees and in groves of walnut and hickory. But not many people ever find its cocoon. The caterpillar spins the cocoon inside a curled leaf, and when the leaves fall in autumn, the cocoon is well hidden.

If it could count, the cottonwood dagger moth could count its cousins by the

Pink-spotted Hawkmoth

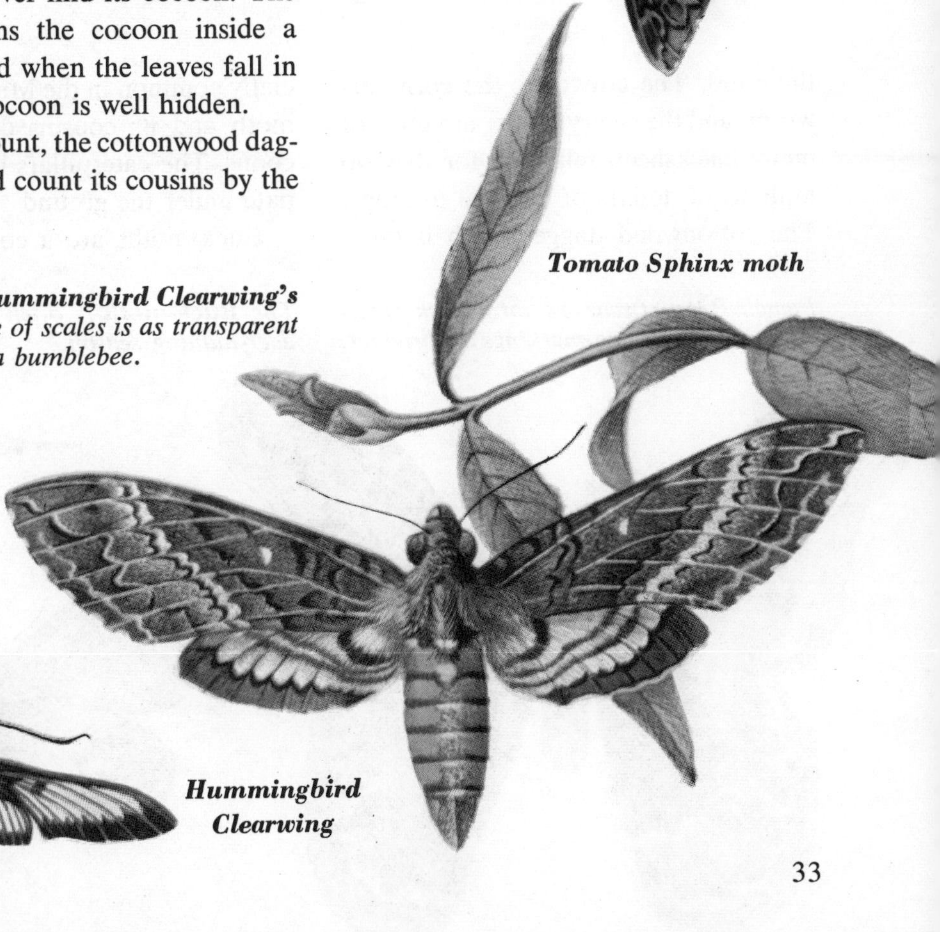

Tomato Sphinx moth

*The part of a **Hummingbird Clearwing's** wing that is free of scales is as transparent as the wing of a bumblebee.*

Hummingbird Clearwing

*The big **Luna** moth is one of the loveliest of all moths and butterflies.*

*The **Cottonwood Dagger** moth belongs to a big family that do not spin cocoons.*

thousand. The cutworm, the corn earworm, and the celery looper are three of many blacksheep relatives, for they do millions of dollars of damage to crops. The cottonwood dagger moth is especially common in the Middle West. This moth and its cousins do not spin cocoons. The caterpillars burrow and pupate under the ground.

Buck-moths are a common sight in

*Female **Prometheas** are not so dark as this male, and their wing-markings are brighter.*

*The **Buck-moth** is often seen during the deer-hunting season.*

many woods on warm fall days. They lay their eggs in clusters on oak twigs. There the eggs stay through winter. The caterpillars that hatch from them in spring remain together and eat in colonies. The wings of the buck-moth are so thinly scaled that light can shine through them.

"Spicebush silk moth" is another name for the Promethea moth. Its caterpillar eats spicebush leaves, but also can be found on sassafras, wild cherry, and tulip trees. The Promethea, the Luna, and the buck-moth are silkworm moths. The moths in this family do not have sucking tubes for sipping nectar. Over the millions of years they have lost mouth parts that most other scalywings have.

Like the Luna, the Promethea spins its cocoon inside a leaf. The caterpillar fastens the cocoon to a twig with long silk threads. The cocoon stays on the tree all winter like a last leaf dangling in the wind.

The front wings of the sweetheart underwing blend so perfectly with the bark of trees that the moth is almost invisible when it is resting. The beautiful hind wings are uncovered only when the moth is flying, and then it is much too dark to see the bright colors.

*The **Sweetheart Underwing** is one of the Cottonwood Dagger moth's many cousins.*

Enemies

A caterpillar does not have a very good chance of growing up. Fat, juicy caterpillars make good meals for many other animals.

A bird carrying a caterpillar to the young birds in its nest is a common sight. Young birds have big appetites. And almost every kind of caterpillar is good food for some kind of bird. Farmers are glad to have birds nest on their land, to help destroy insect pests.

Lizards, too, find some caterpillars good eating. So do toads and frogs. In tropical forests caterpillars have enemies that they do not have in cooler regions. Many are eaten by monkeys. And in parts of Central and South America people cook and eat some kinds of caterpillars. Of course, people are enemies of caterpillars for still another reason. Every year they kill billions of them in their war against insect pests which destroy their crops.

Other insects are enemies, too. Some beetles catch so many caterpillars that

The Scarlet Tanager catches many caterpillars for its young.

The larva of a caterpillar hunter seizes the caterpillar of a ***Gypsy*** *moth.*

they are known as "caterpillar hunters." The larvas of these beetles are also greedy for caterpillars.

The white-faced hornet uses caterpillars as food for the young hornet larvas in its nest. When a hornet finds a big caterpillar, it cuts it up and carries the pieces back to the nest. Some of the hornet's small wasp relatives often lay their eggs in or on a caterpillar. When the eggs hatch, the little larvas feed on the caterpillar and even spin their cocoons on it. Of course, the caterpillar soon dies. Some small wasps even lay their eggs inside the tiny eggs of some butterflies and moths.

Never in all their lives, from egg to winged adult, are the scaly-wings really safe. Their worst enemies of all are the microscopic living things that live in and on them, and cause disease, which kills them by the thousands.

The Tachnid fly lays eggs on ***Gypsy*** *moth larvae, thus helping mankind to control this pest.*

Hornworms *carrying the cocoons of Braconid wasps on their backs do not live long.*

Right, *the White-faced hornet often brings caterpillars to its young.*

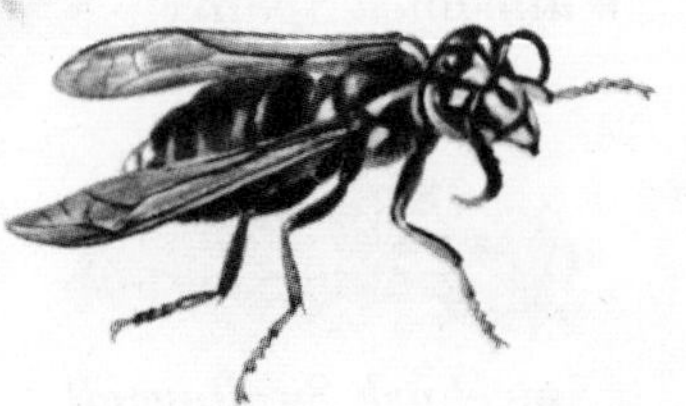

Defense

To save its life a caterpillar cannot fight. Nor can it run away fast. It has other ways of defending itself.

Swallowtail caterpillars may chase enemies away, skunk-fashion. They stick out horns that give out a bad smell. The caterpillar of the spicebush swallowtail also has two big spots on its body that look like eyes. Spots of this kind seem to frighten birds. This caterpillar has still another trick. It builds itself a snug hideaway out of a leaf rolled up and lined with silk. The red admiral caterpillar makes a shelter in a leaf, too, where it hides during the day.

A hornworm is very fierce-looking when it rears up at an enemy. The horn on its body and a sudden sound it makes are frightening, too. Many caterpillars have large horns and menacing ways that seem to scare their enemies.

Hair and spines probably save caterpillar lives, too. Most birds do not eat hairy caterpillars. The Io caterpillar has sharp, stinging spines. An animal that eats this caterpillar is not apt to eat another one soon.

The woolly bear and many other caterpillars may curl up in tight balls and stay very still when enemies are near. Measuring worms lift their bodies almost straight up from a branch and freeze into position. They look almost exactly like twigs.

Adult moths and butterflies can fly away from many of their enemies. But birds can fly much faster and catch them easily. Some scaly-wings have other

*The eyespots of the **Spicebush Swallowtail** caterpillar, the horn of a **Hornworm,** and the stinging spines of the **Io** caterpillar may help protect them from their enemies.*

Hornworm of White-lined Sphinx

Io Caterpillar

Red Admiral

Spicebush Swallowtail

*The **Viceroy** butterfly looks so much like the **Monarch** that it is hard to tell these two butterflies apart.*

ways than wings that probably help protect them from birds. The monarch butterfly is thought to have such a disagreeable taste that most birds leave it alone. The viceroy butterfly does not have a bad taste, but it looks so much like the monarch butterfly that birds that do not eat the monarch are almost sure to leave the viceroy alone, too.

Of course, the viceroy did not choose to look like the monarch. No butterfly can change the color of its wings. The viceroy does not even know what a lucky butterfly it is.

Some scientists think that the big eyespots on the hind wings of certain moths —Polyphemus, for instance—may frighten birds away. When the moth is resting, the eyespots are covered up. But when a bird pecks at it, the moth spreads its wings and the eyespots show. A bird may be so startled at a sudden appearance of these big "eyes" that it will fly away without its meal.

In a setting of flowers, the bright colors of many butterflies and moths blend with the bright colors of the flowers they visit. The colorful hind wings of the sphinx moth on page 40 are not easy to see against a cluster of orange flowers. This moth flies about in the daytime. It and some of its cousins look somewhat like bumblebees. Perhaps this resemblance protects them, for most birds leave bumblebees alone. Many sphinx moths look much like hummingbirds. Birds that are looking for a meal of insects are likely to pass by what may appear to them to be another bird.

Some butterflies and moths have become so expert in the art of camouflage that armies, in time of war, have copied their techniques.

The front wings of the clouded locust moth are almost the color of the bark on locust trees. During the day, when this moth rests on the trunk of a locust tree with its wings folded, it is hard to see. Its enemies can easily pass it by without seeing it at all.

Some scaly-wings in other parts of the world have wings that look like leaves. The veins and even insect-nibbled defects are copied exactly. There are even moths that look like bird droppings. Unless such an insect moves, enemies do not see it as a living creature.

In the life of a butterfly or moth it is just as important to have good ways of protecting the pupa and eggs as the caterpillar and adult.

All their lives the scaly-wings are eaten by their enemies. They would all have disappeared long ago if the females did not lay so many eggs.

When eggs are laid one at a time in different places, there is a good chance that some will not be found and eaten. A mass of eggs laid on a twig may match the color of the bark and look like a swollen part of the twig. Pupas may be wrapped in leaves or lost in leaf piles. Some are underground. Almost all are well hidden in out-of-the-way places, safe from the eyes of their enemies.

***Clark's Day Sphinx** is one of the few moths that fly in bright sunshine.*

The ***Parnassian*** *moth caterpillars use an unattractive scent as a means of defense.*

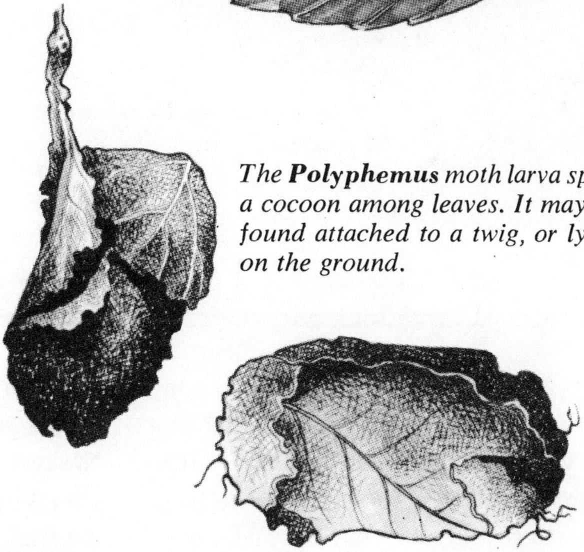

The ***Polyphemus*** *moth larva spins a cocoon among leaves. It may be found attached to a twig, or lying on the ground.*

with wings shut

The bright-colored underwings of the ***Clouded Locust*** *are hidden when the moth rests by day. The covering upper wings almost exactly match the bark of locust trees.*

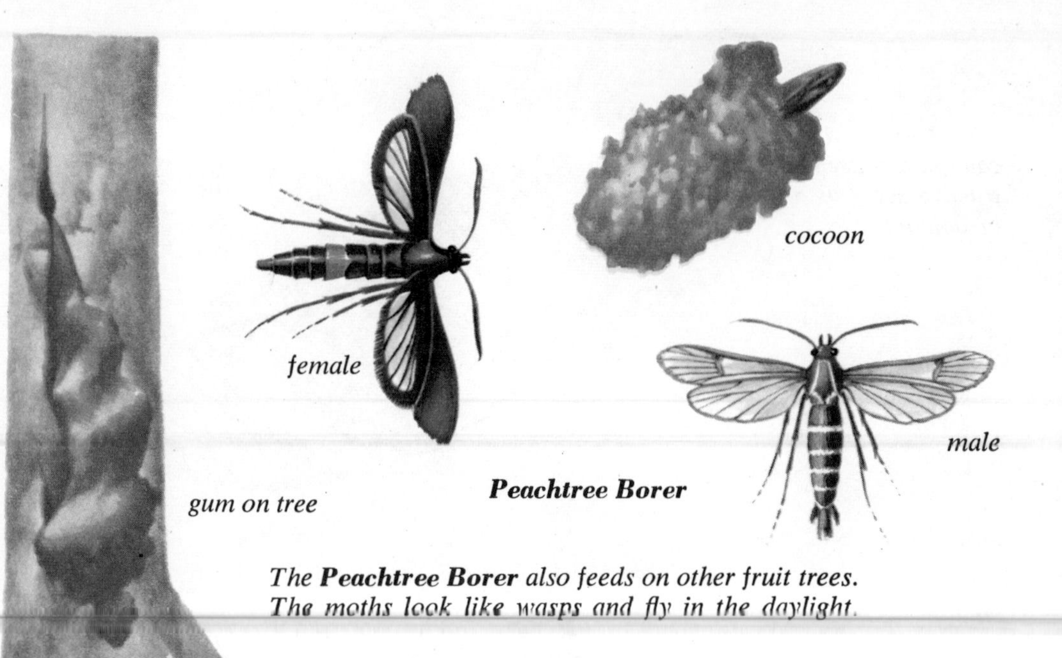

*The **Peachtree Borer** also feeds on other fruit trees.
The moths look like wasps and fly in the daylight.*

Destroyers

In getting food for themselves, many moths and butterflies harm plants that we value, and do other damage. The cabbage butterfly, for example, destroys enormous amounts of cabbage each year. Most of the scaly-wing destroyers, however, are moths, not butterflies. All of these destroyers do the damage they do when they are caterpillars.

The peachtree borer looks much like a small wasp, but it is a moth. It kills or damages thousands of peach trees each year. If peach growers did not protect their trees from it, there might soon be no peaches.

In midsummer the female moth lays hundreds of eggs low on the trunk of a peach tree. The eggs hatch into tiny white larvas that chew their way into the trunk. If there are enough of them, they kill the tree. They do not have to eat their way far into a peach tree to do it great damage. The living, growing cells in the trunk are just inside the bark.

The worm in a wormy apple is not a true worm. Instead, it is the caterpillar of the codling, or codlin, moth. "Codlin" is an old word that means "young apple." The moth gets its name from that word.

The codling moth came to America in colonial days with apple trees the colonists brought with them. Now it is a pest in orchards all over the country.

It is a small moth, hardly more than a quarter of an inch long.

The female moth lays her small white eggs when the trees are still in bloom. She lays them one at a time on the leaves and on the tiny apples that are just beginning to grow in the blossoms. When the eggs hatch, the larvas eat their way into the growing apples. Inside they eat and grow until they are about an inch long. Then they eat their way out again and find hiding places in the bark of the tree. There they spin themselves cocoons and stay for the winter.

Unfortunately for the owners of apple orchards as far north as Virginia, there can be three full generations of codling moths in a single year. In the north there is only one. This scaly-wing pest of apples also feeds on other fruits. It eats pear, quince, and English walnut.

Almost everyone who has picked tomatoes has seen tomato hornworms and has been startled by the sudden clicking sound they often make. These big "worms" are the caterpillars of the tomato sphinx moth. And they have appetites to match their size. By eating the leaves of tomato plants, these big caterpillars seriously damage and reduce the tomato crop.

The corn earworm and the European corn borer do great damage to the corn crop each year. Both are moths. Wormy sweet corn can be blamed on the corn earworm. This pest has two other common names that tell other crops it damages. The names are "cotton bollworm" and "tomato fruitworm." The corn borer does its damage by boring into the stalks of corn plants. In less than 50 years it has become one of the worst of

*The **Codling** moth's caterpillar, the **Appleworm,** is found in apples all over the United States.*

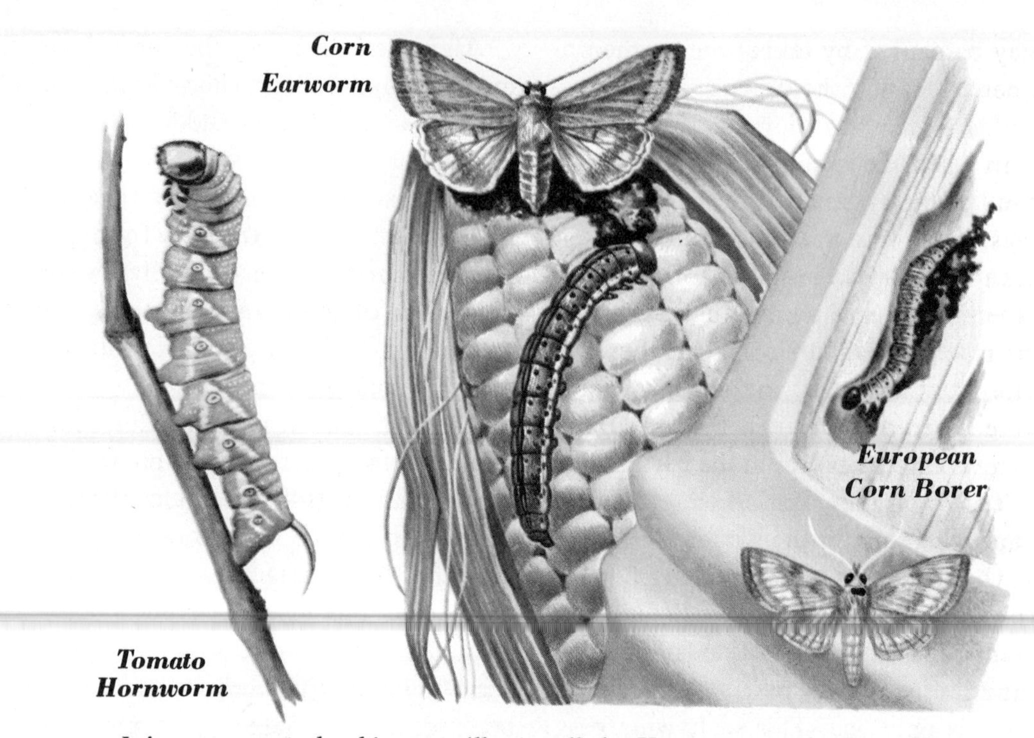

*It is easy to see why this caterpillar is called a **Hornworm.** The **Corn Earworm** and the **European Corn Borer** are two of the farmer's worst enemies.*

all the insect destroyers on American farms. The cost of spraying their fields with insecticides, as well as the loss of many plants, costs the farmers thousands of dollars every year.

The tent caterpillar and the fall webworm are both moths. Many people think that they are closely related because they both spin webs. But they are not. Both moths, however, damage orchard trees as well as trees in woods and parks and yards.

During the summer the female tent caterpillar moth lays her eggs in clusters on the twigs of trees. Often she lays them on apple or wild cherry trees. Early in spring the eggs hatch and the little caterpillars begin spinning a tent together. They leave the tent to eat leaves, but they all come back to it at night and in rainy weather.

The fall webworm builds its tents in the fall. Its tents are built around leaves. The caterpillars do not have to leave their tent to eat. They spend the winter as pupas hidden in crevices in the bark.

The gypsy moth has done millions of dollars' worth of damage to the trees of New England. It has done great damage partly because it has not had enough natural enemies to keep it in check. Its story helps us see how much trouble may be caused by taking an animal to a new region, without considering how it may be kept under proper control.

In 1869 a Frenchman brought with him to Massachusetts some gypsy moth eggs. In Europe this moth is not a serious pest. The man wanted the eggs for experiments he was making. Some of the moths that came from the eggs escaped to the woods. Before long there were so many gypsy moths that they were killing trees by the hundreds.

The gypsy moth is especially troublesome because its caterpillar eats the leaves of all kinds of broadleaf trees and of some evergreens. It would be even harder than it is to control if the female moth could fly about. She has wings, but she does not use them. She lays her eggs not far from the pupal case she comes from.

Tussock moths are relatives of the gypsy moth. The white-marked tussock moth is found over the country from the Rockies eastward. Its caterpillars and its cocoons are a common sight on streets lined with shade trees. The sticky bands painted on the trunks of city trees are helps in controlling this destroyer. In the great timber forests of the Northwest, the Douglas-fir tussock moths eat their way through thousands of valuable trees every year.

Probably not many people would guess, when they saw a female tussock moth, that they were looking at a moth

*The tents of the **Fall Webworm** are built around leaves, not in the forks of twigs as those of the **Tent Caterpillar** are.*

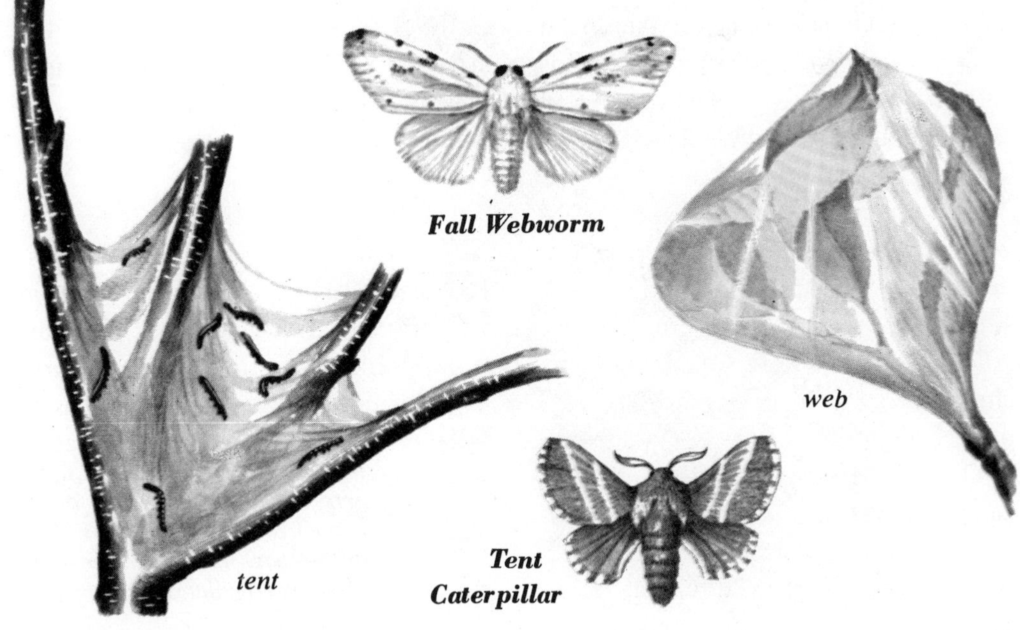

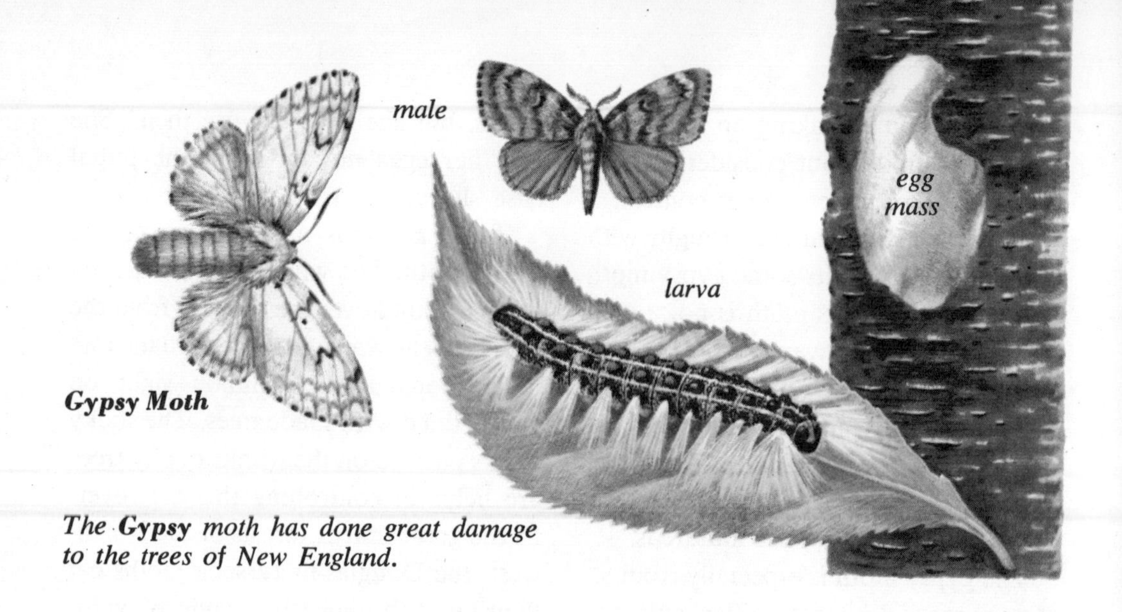

*The **Gypsy** moth has done great damage to the trees of New England.*

at all. For the female, as the picture at the bottom of the page shows, has no wings at all. Of course, without wings, she cannot fly about. When she comes out of her cocoon, she lays her eggs on or near the cocoon. She dies soon afterward. If so many little tussock caterpillars were not blown far and wide by the wind as they dangle on long silk threads they spin, the tussock moth would not spread so easily and be the serious pest that it is.

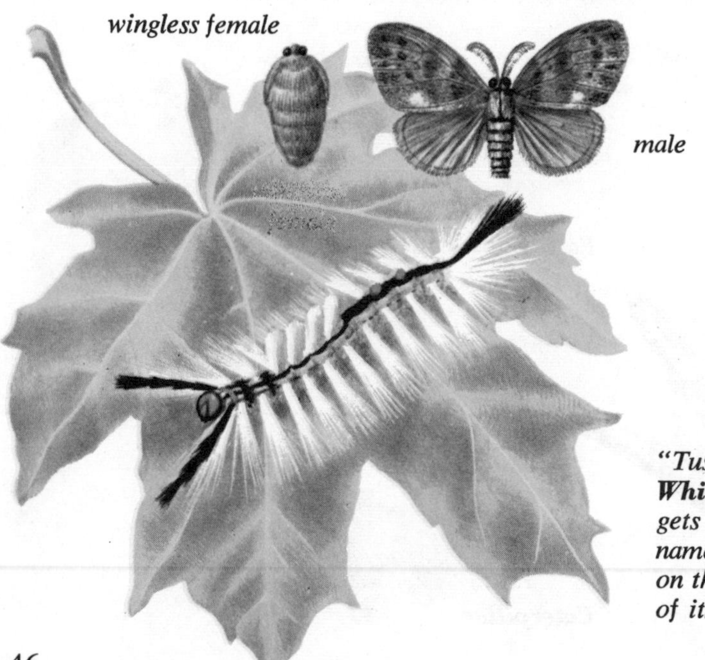

*"Tussock" means "tuft." The **White-Marked Tussock** moth gets the "tussock" part of its name from the thick tufts of hair on the back and down the sides of its caterpillar.*

Like the ***Five-Spotted Hawk-moth,*** *many moths and butterflies help seeds to form by carrying pollen from flower to flower.*

Balance in Nature

No kind of animal is really independent. Each one has its place in a food-chain. Moths and butterflies as a rule eat plant food and in turn are eaten by other insects and birds. But eating and being eaten is not the whole story of the part moths and butterflies play in a community of living things.

The five-spotted hawkmoth has a very long sucking tube. With it the moth can reach down into the flower of a trumpet vine to get nectar. As the moth goes from flower to flower for nectar, it gets pollen on its body from the flowers. As it enters another flower some pollen is brushed off on the sticky part of the flower's pistil. The pistil contains the ovules—the beginnings of seeds. The pollen helps the ovules become seeds.

Many moths and butterflies carry pollen. There is a partnership between the yucca and a little white moth that carries its pollen. The moth, in return for carrying pollen from flower to flower, gets a safe place for its eggs and food for its caterpillars. For the female moth

Yucca Skipper

Harvester

The caterpillar of the **Yucca Skipper** *bores into the roots of yucca plants. The* **Harvester** *is sometimes called a "carnivore" because its caterpillar is a meat eater.*

lays eggs in the pistil. When the eggs hatch, the caterpillars begin eating the seeds around them. But some seeds are left to start new yucca plants.

The caterpillars of the yucca skipper get their food from yucca plants, too. But here the yucca gets nothing in return for the food it furnishes.

Not all scaly-wings are vegetarians. The clothes moth, as everyone knows, is not. A few moths and butterflies help to keep other insects in check. The caterpillar of the harvester butterfly, for instance, eats plant lice.

There are some strange partnerships between scaly-wings and other insects. Ants, for example, take care of caterpillars of the spring azure butterfly. In return the caterpillars serve as "cows" for the ants, giving off a sweet liquid.

In a plant-animal community the numbers of plants and animals stay, as a rule, about the same. There is, scientists say, a balance in nature. Knowing something about the food, the enemies, and the ways of life of scaly-wings may help you see how balance and unbalance come about.

The adult **Clothes** *moth,* left, *does no harm but its larvae may feed on clothing for a year. The* **Spring Azure,** above, *forms an unusual partnership with ants.*

Wintertime

Moths and butterflies are cold-blooded animals. All insects are. They cannot move about in cold weather. As a rule, the adults die when winter comes, and leave behind their eggs or larvas or pupas.

Many moths live through winter in the egg stage. But most scaly-wings hibernate as pupas or as larvas. To hibernate, a caterpillar may build a silk-lined cradle for itself out of a leaf. Some that live in groups spin tents that cover all of them together. But most caterpillars crawl off alone into snug hiding places for their winter sleep.

The common hairstreak, the swallowtails, and many of the skippers are among the scaly-wings that survive winter as pupas. So are the giant silk moths and many, many others.

Adult monarch butterflies do not die at the approach of cold weather. They solve the problem of winter as many birds do—they migrate. Every fall the

*The **Banded Woolly Bear** and the caterpillar of the **Viceroy** hibernate when winter comes. **Common Sulphurs** hibernate either as pupas or as larvae.*

Great flocks of ***Monarch*** *butterflies are a common sight in fall. They are among the few butterflies which migrate when cold weather comes.*

monarchs gather in great groups and fly south. In spring they fly north again.

The pretty painted lady is another butterfly that gathers in flocks and migrates. But its migration does not always have anything to do with cold weather. Some scientists think that it migrates whenever there come to be too many in a region. This butterfly may be the most widely distributed of all butterflies. At any rate, it is found in a great many parts of the world. The painted lady has another way of spending the winter—it hides away and hibernates.

The buckeye, mourning cloak and anglewings are other butterflies that hibernate as adults and wait for warmer days. The few butterflies that do are seen early in spring some time before other butterflies and moths appear.

The red admiral, too, may pass the winter as an adult hidden in some crevice in the rocks or in a hollow tree. Or it may, instead, live through cold weather as a pupa. Often the chrysalis is in the silk-lined leaf shelter the caterpillar made to hide in.

Scaly-wings are creatures of the summer season. But all through wintertime, unseen in cracks and crannies all around us, billions of them hide as eggs or caterpillars, as pupas or adults, and wait for summer to come again.

Gray Hairstreak

*The **Gray Hairstreak** gets its name from the thin tails on its wings.*

Spicebush Swallowtail

*The **Swallowtails** are the largest North American butterflies.*

Parnassius

***Parnassians** are related to the **Swallowtails,** but lack the distinctive wing "tail."*

*The **Red Admiral** hibernates either as a chrysalis or as an adult butterfly.*

*The **Painted Lady** finds a hidden nook and stays motionless through the winter.*

TABLE OF ILLUSTRATED BUTTERFLIES AND MOTHS

Scientists have found and named more than 20,000 different kinds of butterflies and four times that many moths. This table gives the names of only those few moths and butterflies that are pictured in this book, and groups them according to family. The numbers after the common names are page numbers that tell where to find the pictures.

FAMILY	COMMON NAME	SCIENTIFIC NAME	FOOD
	Monarch 22, 23, 27, 50	Danaus plexippus	Milkweed
	Zebra 4, 5, 10	Heliconius charitonius	Passion flower
	Gulf fritillary 4, 5	Agraulis vanillae	Passion flower
	Variegated fritillary 4, 28	Euptoieta claudia	Pansy, passion flower
	Regal fritillary 28	Speyeria idalia	Violet
	Diana fritillary 6	Speyeria diana	Violet
	Great Spangled Fritillary 15		
NYMPHALIDAE *Brush-footed Butterflies*	Checkerspot 28	Euphydryas chalcedona	Monkey flower
	Question-mark 10, 23	Polygonia interrogationis	Elm, hop, nettle
	Comma 27	Polygonia comma	Hop, elm, nettle
	Mourning cloak 17	Nymphalis antiopa	Willow, other trees
	Red admiral 38, 51	Vanessa atalanta	Hop, nettle
	Painted lady 51	Vanessa cardui	Burdock, thistle
	Buckeye 27	Precis coenia	Gerardia, plantain
	Banded purple 6	Limenitis arthemis	Willow, aspen
	Red-spotted purple 15	Limenitis astyanax	Willow, aspen
	Viceroy 39, 49	Limenitis archippus	Willow, aspen
	Pearly-eye 21	Lethe portlandia	Grasses
	Common wood nymph 29	Cercyonis alope	Grasses
	Common hairstreak 29	Strymon melinus	Hop, nettle
LYCAENIDAE *Hairstreaks, Coppers, and Blues*	Gray hairstreak 51	Feniseca tarquinius	Aphids on alder
	Harvester 48	Lycaena hypophlaeus	Sorrel, yellow dock
	American copper 29	Lycaenopsis pseudargiolus	Dogwood
	Spring azure 6	Everes comyntas	Legumes
	Eastern tailed blue 29	Leptotes marina	Legumes
	Western pygmy blue 10	Brephidium exilis	Lamb's-tongue
PIERIDAE *Sulphurs and Whites*	Cabbage butterfly 10	Pieris rapae	Cabbage family
	Cloudless sulphur 6	Phoebis eubule	Legumes
	Southern dog-face 10	Zerene caesonia	Lead plant
	Common sulphur 29, 49	Colias philodice	Clover
PAPILIONIDAE *Parnassians and Swallowtails*	Parnassian 6, 41, 51	Parnassius smintheus	Sedum
	Black swallowtail 20, 29	Papilio polyxenes var. asterias	Carrot, parsley
	Giant swallowtail 20	Papilio cresphontes	Citrus, prickly ash
	Tiger swallowtail 12, 20	Papilio glaucus	Wild cherry
	Spicebush swallowtail 38, 51	Papilio troilus	Sassafras, spicebush
	Zebra swallowtail 7, 20	Papilio marcellus	Pawpaw
	Silver-spotted skipper 30	Epargyreus clarus	Locust
	Common sooty-wing 31	Pholisara catullus	Lamb's-quarters
HESPERIIDAE *Skippers*	Sleepy dusky-wing 31	Erynnis brizo	Oaks
	Arctic skipper 6, 30	Carterocephalus palaemon	Grasses
	Cloudy Wing 30		
	Roadside skipper 31	Amblyscirtes vialis	Grasses
	Brazilian skipper 31	Calpodes ethlius	Canna
	Yucca skipper 48	Megathymus yuccae	Yucca

MOTHS			
FAMILY	COMMON NAME	SCIENTIFIC NAME	FOOD
SPHINGIDAE *Sphinx Moths*	Pink-spotted hawkmoth 33	Herse cingulata	Sweet potato
	Tomato sphinx 23, 33, 44	Phlegethontius sexta	Tomato, tobacco
	Five-spotted hawkmoth 47	Phlegethontius quinquemaculatus	Tobacco, tomato
	Blinded sphinx 9	Paonias excaecatus	Rose family
	Hummingbird clearwing 33	Hemaris thysbe	Viburnum
	Gaudy sphinx 11	Pholus labruscae	Grape family
	Clark's day sphinx 40	Prosperpinus clarkiae	
	Striped morning sphinx 9	Celerio lineata	General feeder
SATURNIIDAE *Silkworm Moths*	Ailanthus 23, 25, 26	Philosamia walkeri	Ailanthus
	Cecropia 18, 23	Platysamia cecropia	Apple, willow, other trees
	Promethea 23, 34	Callosamia promethea	Spicebush, sassafras
	Luna 20, 23, 34	Actias luna	Walnut, persimmon
	Polyphemus 16	Telea polyphemus	Various trees
	Io 11, 38	Automeris io	Various trees
	Buck-moth 34	Hemileuca maia	Oaks
CITHERONIIDAE	Regal moth 32	Citheronia regalis	Various trees
	Imperial moth 9	Eacles imperialis	Various trees
ARCTIIDAE *Tiger Moths*	Leopard moth 9	Ecpantheria deflorata	Plantain
	Fall webworm 45	Hyphantria cunea	Various trees
	Isabella tiger moth 23, 49	Isia isabella	Plantain
	St. Lawrence tiger moth 32	Parasemia parthenos	Low plants
NOCTUIDAE	Cottonwood dagger moth 34	Acronicta lepusculina	Cottonwood
	Corn earworm 44	Heliothis armigera	Corn
	Sweetheart underwing 35	Catocala amatrix	Willow, poplar
	Clouded locust 41	Euparthenos nubilis	Locust
	Black witch 8	Erebus odora	Acacias
LIPARIDAE	White-marked tussock moth 46	Notolophus leucostigma	Shade trees
	Gypsy moth 37, 46	Lymantria dispar	Shade trees
GEOMETRIDAE *Measuring Worm Moths*	Fall cankerworm 11, 21	Alsophila pometaria	Fruit, shade trees
AEGERIIDAE	Peachtree borer 42	Conopia exitiosa	Peach
PYRALIDAE	European corn borer 44	Pyrausta nubilalis	Corn
	Codling moth 42	Carpocapsa pomonella	Apple, pear

Index

Ailanthus, 23, 25, 26
American copper, 29
Arctic skipper, 6, 30

Banded purple, 6
Black swallowtail, 20, 29
Black witch, 8
Blinded sphinx, 9
Brazilian skipper, 31
Buckeye, 27
Buck-moth, 34

Cabbage butterfly, 10
Cecropia, 18, 23
Checkerspot, 28
Clark's day sphinx, 10
Clouded locust, 41
Cloudless sulphur, 6
Codling moth 42
Comma, 27
Common hairstreak, 29
Common sooty-wing, 31
Common sulphur, 29, 49
Common wood nymph, 29
Cottonwood dagger moth, 34

Diana fritillary, 6

Eastern tailed blue, 29
European corn borer, 44

Fall cankerworm, 11, 21
Fall webworm, 45
Five-spotted hawkmoth, 47

Gaudy sphinx, 11
Giant swallowtail, 20
Gulf fritillary, 4, 5
Gypsy moth, 37, 46

Harvester, 48
Hummingbird clearwing, 33

Imperial moth, 9
Io, 11, 38
Isabella tiger moth, 23, 49

Leopard moth, 9
Luna, 20, 23, 34

Monarch, 22, 23, 27, 50
Mourning cloak, 17

Painted lady, 51
Parnassian, 6, 41, 51
Peachtree borer, 42
Pearly-eye, 21
Pink-spotted hawkmoth, 33
Polyphemus, 15, 22
Promethea, 23, 34

Question-mark, 10, 23

Red admiral, 38, 51
Red-spotted purple, 15
Regal fritillary, 28
Regal moth, 32
Roadside skipper, 31

Silver-spotted skipper, 30
Sleepy dusky-wing, 31
Southern dog-face, 10
Spicebush swallowtail, 38
Spring azure, 6
St. Lawrence tiger moth. 32
Striped morning sphinx, 9
Sweetheart underwing, 35

Tiger swallowtail, 12, 20
Tomato sphinx, 23, 33, 34

Variegated fritillary, 4, 28
Viceroy, 39, 49

White-marked tussock moth, 46

Yucca skipper, 48

Zebra, 4, 5, 10
Zebra swallowtail, 7, 20

Eastern Tailed Blue

Bronze Copper

American Copper

Purplish Copper

D